EVERYTHING ARRIVES AT THE LIGHT

EVERYTHING ARRIVES
AT THE LIGHT

Lorna Crozier

M&S

Canadian Cataloguing in Publication Data

Crozier, Lorna, 1948-
Everything arrives at the light

Poems.

ISBN 0-7710-2479-7

I. Title.

PS8555.R79E84 1995   C811'.54   C94-932593-7
PR9199.3.C76E84 1995

The publishers acknowledge the support of the Canada
Council and the Ontario Arts Council for their publishing
program.

Lines from "Anthem" by Leonard Cohen, which appear on
page *vii*, are reprinted by permission of Leonard Cohen and
Leonard Cohen Stranger Music, Inc.

Typesetting by M&S, Toronto

Printed and bound in Canada on acid-free paper

McClelland & Stewart Inc.
The Canadian Publishers
481 University Avenue
Toronto, Ontario
M5G 2E9

1 2 3 4 5   99 98 97 96 95

For Donna Bennett, editor and friend

There is a crack in everything.
That's how the light gets in.

– Leonard Cohen

Enter my darkness, I give you
My darkness;
Together for one second we are light.

– Gwendolyn MacEwen

Contents

I

Halfway to Heaven

Be watchful, and strengthen the things that remain, that are ready to die.

– Revelation 3:2

Where does that singing start, you know,
that thin sound – almost pure light?
Not the birds at false dawn or their song
when morning comes, feathered throats
warm with meaning. A different kind of music.

Listen, it is somewhere near you.
In the heart, emptied of fear,
stubbornly in love
with itself at last, the old
desires a ruined chorus,
a radiant, bloody choir.

Where does the singing start?
Here, where you are, there's room
between your heartbeats,
as if everything you have ever been
begins, inside, to sing.

Naming the light as the Inuit
the snow. The light around my father's

hands as he lay dying, his worn
fingers curled. Unborn animals, sleeping.

Womb-light and the glow of dreams,
they slow you down like water.

My father's body flew up in smoke,
ashes under my nails. Ten moons

rose from my fingers above the lake
where we scattered him,

the shore luminous with alkali
and lichen-splattered stones.

His brief shining in the air
I hold to me now in this place

where winter nights are darkest
because there is no snow.

The blue spruce all lean
in one direction. Without philosophy.
Nothing to push them this way or that
except the wind. Beyond the shelterbelt
some farmer planted forty years ago,
wheat rolls to the horizon and doubles back,
each kernel the soul of one newly dead
resting in the field as an animal will rest
before it heads for home.

The road I run borders the monastery.
Ahead of me a black man walks, reading
a book, monk or not, it's hard to tell.
He must be from a warmer place, he wears
a jacket though it isn't cold,
a red wool cap. I hope he's a missionary
come from far away to make us pagan.
I am ready to be fox or wild cat,
to lift like a crow into high blue boughs,
my nest of sticks dancing in the wind.
I am tired of this heaviness, sick of sorrow,
the sounds we make to give the world
a human shape.

       O, to lean in one direction,
to know the sky the way a tree knows it,
halfway to heaven, inarticulate,
the dead among the green wheat
holding their tongues.

The name is mimulus. We've been trying
to remember all winter and suddenly
I find it in a book called *Human Wishes*.
Last July I bought a basket
for our porch where the yellow
bloomed, though we ourselves
lacked beauty here, not wanting
what the sea was offering or the loss
of brightness in the air. The cat, too,
missed his alley in Saskatoon and spoke out
loudly against the rain. To our neighbours
I had to explain the language
we brought with us: *magpie, slough,
caragana, brome*. I had to tell
the story of my friend.

Last summer he came from Toronto
to gather wildflower seeds
on the farm where he grew up,
the seeds, older than his absence,
so deep they went in his memory.
Weak with illness, a month before he died
he planted them outside his apartment
among the weeds in sidewalk cracks.
Imagine the abundance of that gesture,
the frail human planting, his longing
for his childhood blooms.

Mimulus is the one we've been seeking,
trying to begin a tradition here
so we can say in long evenings

to our friends, "Every summer
in our porch we hang mimulus,"
memory and small half-spoken wishes
making out of flowers another home.

I am beginning to understand Virginia Woolf's
suicide.
        Tonight the river looks so forgiving.
And there is always room for a woman
walking, slow. She stepped
without pause
          into the river's cold garden,
stones in her pockets;
floating above the water,
her fine-boned face, a bloodless moon.

Once so far out there's no turning,
and I want to believe
the birds she heard speak Greek
followed her out, past the lights
of the houses, burning,
before the stones pulled her down.

Some nights when I walk alone along the shore,
my own death heavy inside me,
I think I see a huge fish
          break the surface,
scatter the minnowy light.

Dark-scaled and ancient,
I know he is the one who dragged himself
for years across her dreams to meet her,
the one who swallowed her,
ferried her in his journey to the sea.

He must be surprised sometimes
at the images that surface in his cold brain
– the phantom limbs,
the small feet in stockings,
                    words, words, words
and the Greek that bubbles
from his huge toothless mouth
as if he talked to birds
and the birds talked back.

I've been crying a week
over the cat. There are some
I can say this to and others
I cannot. *He's only a cat,*
many reply. I now divide
people into these two camps.
It's one way of knowing the world.

Meanwhile the cat is
at the vet's in a small cage
and will not eat. *Cats
are the first anorexics,*
my brother writes from Calgary.

I keep hearing the cat
around the house. The first time
it's a wisteria pod
rubbing against the window pane
the way a cat will rub
around your legs. Then it's
my mother-in-law breathing.
She's emphysemic and at night
hisses when she exhales.

The cat used to sit
at the bottom of our bed
when we made love
and when my husband came,
the cat would meow
though I was the noisy one,
and sometimes

he'd even nip my husband's heel.
Pain and pleasure, it's become
an addiction in our house.

When I start crying on the phone
my mother tries to comfort me
in that strange way she has.
Animals have it lucky,
you can always put them under,
stop the suffering. I know
she's thinking of my father,
those last months in the hospital.
Never one for understatement
he begged the doctor –
Why don't you just cut my throat?

At seventy-five
she's also trying to tell me
something about herself,
but what can I do?

Right now it's the cat
I'm sad about. He's not
my mother or father,
he's not my husband,
brother, mother-in-law,
or the child I never had.

He's only a cat,
and so I write
this poem for him
with my whole family in it
to bring him home.

I am the one who comes after,
washes the baby or corpse,
comforts the weeping husband, the mother
with no child in her arms.
My cat bore her kittens
without a sound, brought them to me
only when their eyes were open.

My father's eyes in the hospital
were so blue. That afternoon
he gave me such a look
when I told him I'd be back tomorrow.
He died that night.

A year ago, I was on my way
to Kingston to see a friend,
cancer eating her mouth and tongue.
Her husband left a message
at my hotel somewhere near Kenora.
It's too late.
                One night I slept
by a barn, waiting for a sow
to give birth, but the pig man
thought I was there for him
and I couldn't stay. The animal smell
of his hands made me die a little.

In my dreams children, some
with the plush feet of lions,
the faces of dogs,
push through narrow doors,

not the bone arches of my body,
and tug at me
for what they need to grow.

I remember my own birth,
tumbling forward
toward the light the dying speak of,
and I seemed to be there
in that bright room
after
everything had happened,
my mother mended,
the smell of blood completely gone.

Food poured out of his nose
when my father tried to eat.
Milk at first, then pudding,
mashed potatoes, flapper pie.
At breakfast my mother and I
willed some porridge to stay inside,
sneak past the tumours in his throat.

All through that time
as he grew small, over again,
only his hands holding on to their size,
he told the same story – as a kid
he ate three helpings on the farm,
every Sunday with pork or chicken,
a whole can of corn, a loaf
of boughten bread until he fell
under the table with the dog
and rolled in delicious agony,
his belly hard as if he'd swallowed
a burlap sack of stones.

In the hospital, two tablespoons
consumed, he scraped the rest
into the trash by his bed, a funny smile
on his face when he gave the nurse
an empty plate. To please her,
I thought, to make her happy,
a mother with a fussy child, she
the one who kept on saying
He's looking good today,
an ally in the argument

he was having with my mother
who told him he wasn't coming home.
The nurse said, *What an appetite!*
I could have hit her.

At the stove when I was little
he'd add milk to a can of tomatoes,
lots of salt, a little pepper,
and call it soup,
the only thing he ever cooked.
Because I loved him I pretended
it was wonderful, his speciality.
Later I'd pour it down the toilet,
tomato skins like clots of blood
spat into the bowl.

Now I know it was a game they played,
my father and the nurse.
She let him open the door
to the kitchen on the farm,
its windows steamed from cooking,
four milk pails by the sink
waiting to be washed,
at the table the boy
all mouth and gut and growing.

The pain here, a fullness,
not the other kind,
as he licked clean his plate
and held it out to her,
always wanting more.

During drought, wind in the corn stalks
makes the sound of rain. It is comforting
to sit there, and startling to come upon
a wild delphinium in the aspen grove,
a shock of blue, almost pain.
My niece didn't understand the laughter
that followed the scattering of my father's ashes.
Or the place, the desolation –
an alkali lake edged with muck and salt,
no trees to speak of.
It sat at the bottom of the hill
my mother's family used as a garbage dump,
husks of cars and broken whisky bottles,
old combines waiting for a phantom crop.
Patrick found a rusted chain, two-feet long,
with a hook on either end. Called a Come-Along,
he said. My brother and he had brought shovels
to dig up prickly pears for their gardens.
Mom thought it silly – with all their spines
they're pernicious on the prairies.
Not a plant anyone should grow at home.
She wanted to take nothing back,
nor did I,
though bits of my father remained
beneath my fingernails. The next summer
on the Coast, Patrick hung a Japanese lantern
from the chain, hooked the other end
over a branch of our cherry tree. At night
we sometimes light a candle, the lantern's filigree
designed a thousand years ago to keep a flame
alive in the strongest wind or rain.

Just after sunset at ripening time
the candle flame is not as bright
as the few globes of cherries
the birds have left,
though it gives their red an extra glow.

You were black-haired and young
when I first saw you looking from a window
in a village made entirely of wood.
You watched the soldiers as they passed
in their drab, dusty wool.
You may have been crying. I was not
close enough to see, but you raised
the corner of your apron
perhaps to wipe your face or wave
your woman's flag of simple
unbleached cotton, cloth of weariness,
sadness and regret.

I don't know where I was,
if I was the soldier who caught your eye
or that other girl, prepubescent,
carrying a pail in front of her small body
with both hands, willing the milk
not to spill. You turned away then,
pounded with your fists that disappeared
into the dough the way a man is lost
inside a woman's flesh. Always
I connect you with the smell
of yeast, the pale globes rising.
When they lay me in your arms,
the birthcord hanging,
I knew I'd seen your face before.

Father came from a different country,
no trees for building,
just scrub bush and fields of stone.

Perhaps that's why the two of you
never fit together, like the corners
of a badly folded map. The soldier
you watched from the window
had walked too far into the future
without you to ever come back.

The walls of your house
leaned on the wind when Father arrived,
and owls with faces shaped like hearts
nested in the barn behind the tree
where your sister used to swing.

Milk turning sour on her legs,
she pumped her lean body
from leafy shadows into the sun,
dark to light   light to dark
as I moved from where I was waiting
to see once again your face.

You lay completely open,
after birth,
the hands that held me
smelling of warm golden
rounds of bread.

PHOTOGRAPH, NOT OF ME OR LITTLE BILLIE, CIRCA 1953

My mother stands with her bowling team,
she and three neighbour ladies
all in dresses, nothing fancy,
unless it's her buttons
black and shaped like pansies, later
my favourite in the button jar.
If you look at me, then back
at the four young women
who bowl every Wednesday afternoon,
you'll have a hard time seeing
a resemblance, picking out
my mother. Her face
is softer, in photographs
her smile tentative, uncertain,
as if she were back in a one-room school
and had raised her hand
without an answer.
Her dark hair falls in waves,
for all morning around the house
steel clips have gripped her hair,
all that metal making her head
look like some wonderful machine
for inventing electricity.
Like the others she's wearing
black two-inch heels and stockings
(though you can't see) with a seam.
Soon they'll put on bowling shoes,
each choosing one size smaller
than what they need because the number's

stitched in red on the back,
right where everyone can see.
This is my mother's only outing,
Wednesday afternoon, the bowling alley
four blocks from home. It's the beginning
of the fifties. My father's working
at the horseplant, my older brother,
the hockey star, is at school,
and I, too young to be at home
alone, am already obsessed
with the invisible.
Told to sit quiet on the wooden bench,
an orange pop in my hand,
I'm looking far down the bowling alley
past my mother and her team,
trying to catch sight
of the little man who lives
inside the darkness at the end of the lanes.
My mother said he sits on a shelf
as in a closet or a cave
behind the bowling pins
and his name is Little Billie.
When my mother wets her palms,
dabs them on the rag
and throws her last ball,
its echo rolling
down that long hardwood floor,
the pins explode
and he drops down,
flips them all upright
fast but not impatiently,
bent nearly double,
barely seen. He disappears,

balls roll and crash,
then there he is,
just outside the photograph,
waiting in the dark
to set things right.

Mary is reading recipes:
cinnamon she says again and again,
then sprinkles some from the can
on her fingertips, holds them
to her nose, licks them clean.
This is what she knew before,
the taste and smell, but now
there's this, *cinnamon*
written in her mother's hand
on the index card and *1 tsp.*

Surely here is the story of a life,
the recipes making her see
her mother's hands
sticky with pastry, red from beets,
smelling of vinegar and garlic
or apples and peach.

She has saved this box
since her mother's death
and opened it at night,
her husband and the kids in bed.
For years she ran her fingers
over a butter-smudge, a smear of
molasses that dripped from a spoon.
These she could read,
but now the words!

And it's as if her mother were here
again beside her in the kitchen
measuring *cinnamon*,

that most beautiful of sounds,
while Mary reads out loud
what is needed next
and finds it
newly labelled on the shelf.

From doorways the mothers call
the children in. You hear them every night –
their voices, faithful dogs
sniffing the gravel and the grass,
tugging the sleeve of a jacket
to bring a child home. Light from doorways
builds a bridge at the mothers' feet,
crosses lawns to where the children play
Run Sheep Run and *I wish I may, I wish I might,*
I wish I'd see a ghost tonight.

The mothers call, *Maria, Tommy, Josephine.*
Names drift and swirl like falling snow,
settle on the empty swing,
climb the branches to the small maple house
where no one's home.
Michael, Nancy, come to bed.
Across the grass children run barefoot,
somersault and tumble, legs wet with dew.

The ones who are never called
wait just beyond the lilacs, the garden gate.
Come away, come away. They say the words
you love to hear: *Nightjar. Firefly.*
Honey Possum. Like these they move
with ease through any kind of dark
for after all, they'll tell you,
it's just the light
falling so far into itself
it hasn't reached the bottom yet.

While your mother calls,
they hold the hands of a child
who once was you,
move in ever-widening circles
the way the mind moves –

                    out and out –

sing, *Husha, husha, hush.*

A fear so huge
it pushed the girl from the window
three storeys up.

Thirteen years on earth
                    and suddenly
she knew the air, a daring
graceful thing, then grass
hard as clay.

Her three older sisters
watched her jump without a sound
then picked her up
and carried her to bed.

They didn't call the doctor
until her cramps
and bleeding stopped,
what would have been a child
scooped into a bowl,
thrown in the furnace
in those days of coal and fire.

Imagine the afternoon they waited
in that tall Victorian house
for their father to come home,
demanding reverence, embroidery and hours
of sitting, ankles crossed,
sips of lukewarm tea.

Every Sunday in the parlour
the dead Queen watched them
from above the mantle, beside her
the painting of the Morgan stud
their father broke in Tennessee.
His eyes followed their skirts
whispering on dusty rugs,
their small buttoned shoes.

When their mother spoke
she called him *Sir*,
and sometimes stayed inside
her room for days, indisposed,
until her "unnatural colour" went away.

The youngest one
fell down the stairs,
that's what her sisters said,
tripped on her skirts
(she always moved too fast),
leg snapping like willow sticks,
one, two, three.
                    Silly as any girls
dying to tell a story
yet her sisters kept the secret.

They didn't know
she could have bled to death
or lay forever broken
like the thing inside their mother
that would not heal.

Two months later
she could run on crutches

beside them on the grass
and laugh like a child
at the tricks they played.

She was the one who came back
to nurse him
when their mother died,
twenty years since she'd leapt
from the window, belly
heavy as a stone.

In the room she'd never entered
as a child, she found his name
written in a young man's hand
across the first page of the Bible
that never left his bedside stand.
    A common name
she said out loud and it held
no fear

   imagine
the look on her face
as she changed him in that bed,
he who was so tall and fierce,
who begat and begat –
under her hands
     his flesh
hot as a baby's
burned in coal.

SEEING MY FATHER IN THE NEIGHBOUR'S
COCKATOO

The cockatoo says three things:
"Cookie," "Pretty bird," and
"What a beautiful day!"
Some mornings you don't want to hear
"What a beautiful day!"
but nothing stops him.

His name is Joey. Perhaps because
he wants to be something other
than a bird, he pulls the feathers
from his breast,
his grey and naked skin
what you glimpse between
an old man's buttons.

This trick does much
to make him unattractive
though he's a friendly bird, quite
beautiful when he lifts the yellow
plume on the top of his head.

If you say, "Kiss, Joey, kiss,"
and stroke his feathered cheek,
he'll bunt your hand like a cat
and click his beak. Sometimes
when he's feeling fond he'll curl
his tongue, a thick black snail,
around your finger.

The day my father decides to come back,
he hovers behind Joey's eyes

and looks at me in that way he had
as if he'd left us long before he died
to find a new religion,
or grow cell by cell
into a different species,
tired of his memories, the tumours
in his throat that made him sound
as if he shouted underwater.

No matter how I listened
I could not understand
what he was trying to say.

Now in Joey's voice he cries
"What a beautiful day!"
and looks straight at me,
his eyelids grey and wrinkled.
Then with a wink,
he plucks three feathers from his chest
and lets them fall.

When I come again to my father's house
I will climb wide wooden steps
to a blue door. Before I knock
I will stand under the porchlight and listen.
My father will be sitting in a plaid shirt,
open at the throat, playing his fiddle –
something I never heard in our other life.

Mother told me his music stopped
when I was born. He sold the fiddle
to buy a big console radio.
One day when I was two
I hit it with a stick,
I don't know why, Mother covering
the scratches with a crayon
so Father wouldn't see.
It was the beginning of things
we kept from him.

Outside my father's house
it will be the summer
before the drinking starts,
the jobs run out, the bitterness
festers like a sliver buried
in the thumb, too deep under the nail
to ever pull it out. The summer
before the silences, the small
hard moons growing in his throat.

When I come again to my father's house
the grey backdrop of the photos

my mother keeps in a shoebox
will fall away, the one sparse tree
multiply, branches green with rain.
My father will stand in his young man's pose
in front of a car, foot on the runningboard,
sleeves rolled up twice on each forearm.

I will place myself beside him.
The child in me will not budge
from this photograph,
will not leave my father's house
unless my father as he was
comes with me, throat swollen
with rain and laughter,
young hands full of music,
the slow, sweet song of his fiddle
leading us to my mother's
home.

CROSSING WILLOW BRIDGE

On the farm a willow bridge
though this is Saltspring Island
not Japan. Sometimes it crosses
water, sometimes not. This morning
after rain the ground slides into mud.
My mother and I tread our way
to see the baby llama
in the far pasture. A black Lab
lopes up the path, doubles back.
All energy and muscle
and too much love, he bumps our legs.
He belongs here, the family pet.
This morning he has more to do
with time, how it runs ahead and keeps
returning, our smell on its muzzle,
along its back. I'm afraid
he'll knock my mother over.
Suddenly this winter she's unsteady
on her feet. He runs to her
with a stick, strikes her legs
as if he's a monk and she
a stubborn student, seventy-six
this year. How little time
we have to love each other.
The black dog will not leave
though I shout *No*, bang him with my knee
when he jumps up. Our walk becomes
a journey, the dog,
the winter rains coming on.
My mother's arm in mine, we turn back,
cross the willow bridge. Now

the dog swings round,
gathers everything he is
and flies toward us,
under our feet the water running,
willow branches bending at the sound.

After years in the ring
the white stallion
was put out to pasture with the mares
who found him old as well,
knees and forelegs stiff,
wind no longer running in his mane and tail,
what was light in his bones
turned to clay.

One night the man who trained him,
tugged from sleep by his own
marrow aching, limped to the meadow,
seeking the comfort of horses,
muzzles in his palm, their breath
a balm lapping over him,
a warm and healing stream.

Before he could nicker them to his side,
he stopped. Something silver moved
in the meadow, graceful as wind smoothing
the blue of flax or a woman's fine hair.
Something seemed to grow from his longing.

He held his breath, not to frighten
what was there, and walked
as if the grass were ice
and a sound would pull him under.

Drenched in moonlight, it was the stallion,
crossing one foot in front of the other,
as the man had taught him
with oats and apples, soft strokes of praise.

The brown and golden mares stood still,
almost touching. They and the man,
whose smell they had come to know
like the blood smell of this season's
foals turning inside them,
watched
the stallion in his beauty,
slowly dance.

Because we are mostly
made of water and water
calls to water
like the ocean to the river,
the river to the stream,
there was a time when
children fell into wells.

It was a time of farms
across the grasslands,
ancient lakes
that lay beneath them,
and a faith in things
invisible, be it water
never seen or something
trembling in the air.

We are born to fall
and children fell,
some surviving
to tell the tale,
pulled from the well's
dark throat,
wet and blind with terror
like a calf
torn from the womb
with ropes.

Others diminished into ghosts,
rode the bucket up
and when you drank

became the cold shimmer
in your cup, the metallic
undertaste of nails
some boy had carried
in his pocket
or the silver locket
that held a small girl's
dreams.

In those days people
spoke to horses,
voices soft as bearded
wheat; music lived
inside a stone. Not to say
it was good, that falling,
but who could stop it?

We are made
of mostly water
and water calls to water
through centuries of reason
children fall
light and slender
as the rain.

The small perfection of the blue oranda.
It rises between lily pads and hyacinth

like a dream the water had,
fish born in the moon's tranquil sea.

It swims into your mind
when you are weary

when you have touched
for the last time someone

you have loved and must let go,
just as the eye

releases this minnow-quick
breath from its net

and the water, without parting,
takes it in.

Morning opens like a crimson
poppy on a leggy stem. Too much
brightness. As a girl I stood
at the edge of a glimmering pool,
guarded the children. I blew
a silver whistle on a chain
to break the spell, a voice
from the bottom calling them down.
On the back of their necks
water lay its strange maternal
hands, heavy, without bones.

I watched the children bob
hour after hour,
my skin burned and blistered.
Now sun finds the lines it carved
from eye to jaw, around my mouth,
above my freckled knees. It seeks
them out like glacial melt
pushing the ancient riverbeds
closer to the sea. Soon I'll be
all running light and water.

When I dive in next,
the pool's long muscled throat
will pull me down,
my hair waving above the grate
as if to take root in the earth
under everything.
                        This far from the sun
with a glistening tongue,
I'll sing and sing.

II

Height of Summer

There is no way of telling people that they are all walking around shining like the sun.

– Thomas Merton

FOR THE CHILD WHO IS SCARED OF THE DARK

Remember as you lie
in whatever darkness
finds you

somewhere in a shed
a large round light
glows, and underneath,

a golden pool
dips and bobs,
dozens of chicks

bundled together as if
tied with strings.
Nothing is as warm

as those yellow feathers
under the light
that never goes out.

How soft they are
as you lower your hands
as if to wash

in a basin of water
someone has left
all morning in the sun.

The most beautiful
is the woman behind the camera,
the one who is making
the three children smile. Years later
they'll laugh at the photograph,
the funny hair, the bony knees,
show their adult friends
how sweet they looked
in their Sunday dresses white as wings.

No one will remember the way
the woman looked. Now
as she composes sun and shadow,
the children across the lawn
are as separate from her body
as they'll ever be.

If she could see herself
she'd wonder
what has brought her here –
the ordinary house, the narrow garden,
the lilacs, literal and magical,
insisting their scent into the air.

Everything at this moment
conspires
to make her invisible

at the touch of her finger
her three small daughters
turning into memory

turning into light
and the other side of light

where the brightness
she is
      disappears.

Beautiful, ethereal, like a child
imagined for a play, Dominic
born premature five years ago
still has the look of someone
not ready for this world.

Just before his parents
and their two guests
sit down for dinner,
he places his hands
on the thin woman's belly, says
You are going to have a baby.
The adults laugh.
She has three and, at forty-five,
wants no more.

Like a midget clairvoyant
he walks around the table,
looks her husband in the eye.
Soon you are going to die.
Someone tries to make a joke.
There is nervous laughter.
Mommy, when you and Daddy die,
I'm going to build a house out of your bones
and there I'll raise my children.

He speaks precisely
and with a slight English accent;
white Namibian, he's a boy who's travelled
an ocean and a continent to be here.

After dinner, the man and woman
who began their drive home
with smiles and teasing
now shout at one another.
Who's the father? he demands for the third time.
He's had a vasectomy and she is angry
he won't believe the baby's his
(that is, *if* she's pregnant).
Soon I'll be dead anyway, he says,
I guess it doesn't matter.

In his room Dominic lights birthday candles
to place in his mother's skull
where her eyes used to be.
She is calling from downstairs.
Do you have your pyjamas on?
I'm coming up at the count of three.

Dominic tucks his children inside
his mother's head. The rubber mouse named Mimi,
the velvet kangaroo with a penny in its pouch,
the armadillo no bigger than a walnut shell.
One. Two. Three! Dominic stares through
the small round windows at his babies
in their beds. *Sleep*, he says, and breathes
his warm breath over them. *Sleep.*
Bone houses are so cold.

Some say it started
when she was twelve,
with a lighter at the beach
she turned an aerosol
can into a torch,
aimed it at the lake,
the closest vulnerable thing
her hand. It sucked in flames
as if it were born
to carry fire.
That should have been
the lesson.

Eight months later
at the outdoor rink
she tossed lit matches
at an Oilers' jacket
till the ribbing
on the cuff caught fire.
The boy inside it
looked at her
as no one ever had.

There were the usual
singed aureoles of cigarettes
on her shirts and sweaters.
A white crescent moon
glowed above her wrist
from the stove's electric coil.

When she turned thirteen
her mouth learned to love
the taste of smoke
on someone else's skin,
small tongue flickering
in the red of dashboard lights.

What do you do with such a girl?
You can't just watch her burn.

Her fourteenth summer,
she sits in pools of sun,
scarred hand curled in her lap
as if it were the child
that needs talking to,
the one you know
will break your heart

for she slips so lightly
away from you,
delicate and dangerous
as a flame you'd cup
in your own hands
if the heat could be held there,
if you could keep her from burning
brighter,
faster in the wind.

One teacher made the bad child
crawl under her desk and stay there
till recess. It seems strangely sexual
to him now, the dark, the musky smell of her.
Another made the bad child stand
in a waste-paper basket, pushed
wet gum on the end of his nose.
He stood there till he fainted, keeled over
with a crash. One teacher hit the bad child
with the pointing stick when she spelled
a word wrong in the spelling bee.
Another made the bad child rise,
show the class she had wet herself,
a yellow pool around her desk.
One teacher made the bad child eat his words
till he gagged on paper, mouth blue from ink.
One touched the child, so very bad,
where he wasn't supposed to,
another broke the bad child's toes
when she wouldn't stop skipping,
one cut off the bad child's fingers
because he drummed and drummed his desk.
One chopped the bad child into bits.
We watched her bury the body
beneath the monkey bars
where every winter on the cold metal
bad children leave their tongues.

Inside the schoolhouse,
windows boarded up, the last day's
additions remain on the slate
and the strange letter x.
It is alive and numinous
in this room without children.

A raccoon walks down the aisle
between the wooden desks
like a teacher checking sums.
Above her in the gables, her little ones
wait for their lessons.

This is the hour for geography
in the classroom, the hour of maps
and distances. She will teach them
how far they can travel before
the farm dogs pick up their scent,
and the shortest route to home.

What she will do when it is the hour
for poetry is unknown.

Afterwards, the cloakroom empty,
the bookshelves furred with dust,
on the blackboard the x
glows like the eyes of an animal
when it looks out of darkness
toward any kind of light.

My sister who never followed me
was awkward, yet a graceful
lovely thing. Armless,
her hands sprouted
from her shoulder blades,
fingers splayed into fins.

Round hard buds
blunted legs that never grew
yet in the salty sea
she flipped
and somersaulted,
eyes wide open
and green as light
inside a leaf.

Even then I knew
I'd forget most things
but not my sister
or the underwater cave
where we swam to sleep.

My fingers, each distinct
and whole, no flap
of skin between,
made trails on the soft
enfolding walls
like those a snail will leave
as it eats its way across
the algae-skin of stone.

Guided by the green
of her amazing eyes
bone by bone I drew
our mother's face
so I would know someone
when I had to leave my sister
and learn with awkward grace
to love the world.

THE GAME

So many conversations between
the tall grass and the wind.
A child hides in that sound,
hunched small
as a rabbit, knees tucked
to her chest, head on knees,
yet she's not asleep.

She is waiting with a patience
I had long forgotten,
hair wild with grass seeds,
skin silvery with dust.

It was my brother's game.
He was the one who counted,
and I, seven years younger,
the one who hid.

When I ran from the yard,
he found his gang of friends
and played kick-the-can
or caught soft spotted frogs
at the creek so summer-slow,
who can blame him?

As darkness fell,
from the kitchen door
someone always called my name.
He was there before me
at the supper table;
milk in his glass

and along his upper lip
glowing like moonlight.
You're so good at that, he'd say,
I couldn't find you.

Now I wade through
hip-high bearded grass
to where she sits so still,
lay my larger hand
upon her shoulder.

Above the wind I say,
You're it,
then kneel beside her
and with the patience
that has lived so long in this body,
clean the dirt from her nose and mouth,
separate the golden speargrass from her hair.

A sudden clap of light,
then another,
and I see my mother as a child,
beside her
an old woman in a chair.

Through the window
of the farmhouse
in a lightning flash
I see the girl
turn a handle
on a square wooden box
while the woman rocks,
their eyes bright with fear.

My brother and I never knew
my mother's terror
but the dog picked it up,
acting out what he could smell.
Perhaps he heard the song
running over and over in her head
as he whined and shook,
his eyes stunned
from brown to red
in the sky's cold fire.

Stay back from the window,
my mother said
as we watched the lilacs dance.
To stop our fear, she told us
thunder wakes

the darkness underground
and makes things grow. After
the clouds had cleared
our garden shivered into life.

In the eye of the storm
I see my mother's
small arm – a blur of white –
turning the handle
of the phonograph,
the record spinning round
beneath the needle's bite.

The aunt who should have
cared for her
rocked in a chair, yelled
faster, faster,
the song my mother made
from a child's fear
rose above the storm

while all around her
lightning walked the black fields,
and wheat, trembling underground,
began its fierce journey
toward the sun.

The only thing this town's
got going is the past.
Here the erotics of history,
and vice versa, bring prosperity.
In the Red Onion Saloon
I read what's supposed to be
an amusing tale of the girls upstairs
who worked in "cribs," ten by ten cells,
just enough room to lie
spread-legged. For efficiency

someone built a row of wooden dolls
behind the bar, an iron rod
through their ribs
joining them like paper cut-outs,
below each one
the number of a room.
When one of the girls was occupied
the bartender flipped a doll
onto her back
and when he righted her
another miner climbed the stairs.

The "Red-Rock Ladies" they were called
and on the wall a turn-of-the-century
photograph. Four small-town girls
open-faced and plump
look out at you
like someone in an ad for milk
or someone you used to know,
that quiet girl who caught the bus to school

from Olds or Antelope or Manyberries,
the one who ate her lunch outside alone.

They're in their Sunday best,
long skirts, high collars, all
the buttons buttoned up.
One holds a small dog,
another, a spotted cat.

I think of the ponies
who never got to leave the mines,
some born blind inside,
the stories go,
pulling car after car
in numbing dark. The photographer
has made the Red-Rock Ladies smile (I hope
his words were kind)

but they all look pale,
discomforted,
two with their reluctant pets
tucked into the fleshy curve of their arms,
in the Red Onion
perhaps all they knew
of love.

I used to be such
a swimmer, surface diving
to the loud blue hum around the grates,
following the lines and cracks
that led to a cave I could
never find the entrance to,
ears aching. All summer

without shoes, my feet
brown otters pulled me
from the earth. There was a
birth-gleam all over me,
a loss of language, my mouth
an anemone that opened, closed,
my sex unfurling in the broken
light that stroked me underwater.

Now the ticket window's boarded up
and barbed wire bites
the wooden fence I used to climb
at night to be alone
in the blue-green shimmer
stretched taut by moonlight.

Sometimes a boy dropped
from the darkness
above the diving board
and swam beside me, a strange boy
I'd never seen at school.
We moved together, a pair of wings

unfolding, my new breasts
in his mouth or the mouth of the water.

By late August, beetles fell
from somewhere in the sky,
the click of their bodies
on cement like seconds ticking.
My fingers drummed down his belly
as we counted them.

I splashed and tumbled
through every morning lesson
and told no one
I was there
where I shouldn't have been
at night, beetles falling
like walnuts from a tall black tree.

It was the wild ones you loved best,
the boys who sat surly at the front
where every teacher moved them,
the ones who finished midterms
first, who showed up late,
then never showed at all.

Under the glare of outdoor lights
you watched them bang
their hard bodies against the boards,
gloves and sticks flying.
In the cold they looked back at you
through stitched and swollen eyes,
smiled crookedly to hide
their missing teeth,
breathed through noses broken
in a game or pool-hall fight.
There was always someone older,
a fist and grin
they just couldn't walk away from,
there was always some girl, watching.

They were the first boys you knew
who owned a car, who rolled
a thin white paper, who talked
out of the side of their mouths,
cigarettes burning.
You watched them fall
quick and bright and beautiful
off the highest diving boards,
you watched them disappear

then throw themselves on top of you
till you thought you'd drown.

Oh, they were cool and mean,
but sometimes they treated you
with such extravagant tenderness,
giving you a rhinestone broach
they'd nicked from Woolworth's,
a fuzzy pink angora, giving up
their jackets on an autumn night
to keep you warm. How you loved
to move inside the shape of them,
the smell of sweat and leather
kissing your skin. For months
you wore their hockey rings
wound with gauze and tape
as if one day
you'd need to bind a wound.

The wild boys had the fastest
tongues, the dirtiest jokes,
and told anyone who'd listen
what they'd done to a girl
the night before
though in the narrow darkness
of a car or on a blanket
by the dam where eels slid
just beneath the surface, you knew
you did it to each other
and the words they said were sweet.

The boys you loved
knew everything, guided your mouth
and hands, showed you what you really

wanted from this life. Now,
it is their brokenness
you long to touch, the parts
they left behind or lost

as they learned too soon
too many years ago
what it took and took
to be a man.

I miss the smokers, the heavy drinkers
though my eyes burn when someone lights
a cigarette. I miss the poet who drank
a bottle of gin a day and talked to his
parrot in bird-vowels of squeaks and squawks,
its eyes following his big gentle hands
stumbling through the air. I miss the post-coital
smoke of my lover as he raised two fingers
that smelled of me to his mouth and inhaled
again and again. I miss the whisky priest who danced
wet in his robes in the fountain below the Spanish Steps,
holding a gelato high above his head and
never dropping it. I miss the tin tobacco can
of my sixty-cigarette-a-day mother-in-law who insisted
she didn't inhale. I miss my father who asked me
to smuggle a case of beer into the cancer ward,
who dragged his intravenous stand to the dungeon
smoking room five times a day. I miss the artist
in Zagreb who for over an hour in the bar
tried to touch the mole on my shoulder
and always overshot his mark, his yellow-stained
finger jabbing the air. I miss the beautiful
woman who drank with Dylan Thomas. After three
scotch on ice, she tossed her head all night,
throwing back the long hair she didn't have anymore.
I miss the smokers, the heavy drinkers,
the ones who walked naked through parties,
covered with the host's shaving cream, the ones
who pushed dill pickles into their ears,
who played the harmonica with their noses,
who could aim a smoke ring to settle like a halo

over someone's blessed head. I miss them on the couch
where I covered them with the extra blanket,
where I took the glowing ember from between their fingers.
I miss climbing the stairs to bed, draped in their silky
cape of smoke, their singing and jubilation, the small
bonfires of their bodies burning through
what little was left of the night.

The woman who lay in bed for three days
as if waiting for someone to arrive
had just given birth
to her second baby, a ten-pound boy
(full term, an easy labour),
brain-damaged.
He can breathe but cannot eat.
She was expecting someone else;
she lay there, learning to be
a different kind of mother.

By the dugout on the road I walk
a windmill turns the wind.
Danger. Thin ice, painted on a board
beneath the blades. Today the ice
so thin it's water. Midsummer,
and in the city the daughter of my friend
walks the streets, red-haired and schizophrenic.
There is no comfort, her mother writes,
out of darkness only pain.

The fields of wheat along the road
look thick and lush
but the kernels aren't filling out,
what should be gold stays green.
In this country that yearly battles drought
there's been too much rain.

If my friend were with me
I would tell her of this baby,
the mother who croons his name

so he will know the sound
she calls him by
and answer to it, in whatever dream.

And the father
who goes each night
to the hospital after work
      and sleeps there,
placing his small son on his chest –

                two hearts beating.

It seems to comfort him,
he says, *and me*,
though he knows in the nursery's
strange light, their love
is a letting go,
          a holding,
close and brief as breath.

Having no souls, they have come,
Anyway, beyond their knowing.
— James Dickey, "The Heaven of Animals"

If animals have no souls
it's because they do not need them.
There is something forever about their time
on earth, whether they move on wing, paw or hoof,
or slide with huge, cold bodies
across the blue-green worlds.

Wherever they dwell, their gaze
when they look at you
comes from a great height –
the yellow of hawk and panther eye –
or so close up
they've slipped under the leaves
of your eyelids and stare from the inside out.

In books of the dead the human soul
becomes bird or butterfly
or soft-pawed, graceful thing.
Grant animals a soul: might it not leave
their bodies in the shape of ours?
Assume the best of us, the high forehead,
the shapely arms, the exactitude of
thumb on index finger.

That's what those bright ones are,
those people we glimpse with a glow about them,
an ecstacy. The souls of animals

crossing from one country to another,
pausing for a moment among us
only to rise in glory,
beasts again.

From her small balcony where she hangs the wash, her son's red jumpsuits, her husband's shirts and socks worn thin at the heels, you can hear the zoo just up the hill. The parrots with their jungle tongues, the scream of monkeys, the old lion's cough. She walks up on Sundays, her little boy's hand clutching his cone so hard it almost breaks. From the top of the hill before smog insinuates its yellow between the streets, she can see the stadium crouching like Yeats' huge beast moving its heavy thighs, already born, its belly barely large enough to hold the dead. In their cages the animals press against the bars, hurting themselves, not to see her and the child, but to gain another inch of sky. Strange what we cage, she thinks, what grace we want worn down, what colours muted, what beauty made smaller than our own. Back in the apartment where the cries of the zoo weave her child's dreams of paradise, it is not the panther escaped from its cell she fears, nor the lion prowling the balcony, picking up the smell of her loved ones, mouthing their clothes. It is the fall of the human foot, the creak of ordinary shoes, the sound the hand makes when it is putting things together or tearing them apart. Tonight on the balcony the noise she hears is only the woman who helps with the housework, humming a song she just heard on the radio, taking the washing in, before the rain.

The eyes of Christ and the eyes of the lamb look at me beseechingly from the wall above the desk. The painter had little skill, understanding only the sentimental side of suffering. The lamb hangs around Christ's neck, its head just above his heart, like a fox stole draped across the shoulders of a woman, nose and jaw bobbing against her breasts. The lamb is devoid of character, its body plush and pliable as if someone has stripped it of its bones. You can't look at it without thinking of sacrifice, the noise the knife makes when it slits a throat. Imagining that, your mind then hears a hammer pounding nails and the wet, splintering sound of metal breaking through the bones of hands and feet to meet the wood.

In the hall another Christ: this one could be labelled *After*, for he's been resurrected – his heart flies from his chest like a bird soaked in blood. He holds a green globe in his hand. I think it's supposed to be the earth but it looks more like a bowling ball, and it's not hard to believe that beneath his robe this Christ wears a pair of bowling shoes with the size stitched in leather on the backs of the heels. Just as it's not hard to believe the story my friend tells of a huge crucifix he saw in Texas, the hanging, naked Christ in cowboy boots.

The boots would be what you'd see first, looking up from the ground, and you couldn't help but stop and admire the leather inlay and try to figure out the symbolism in the bootmaker's designs. You'd even start to wonder about the horse and what happened to it. Maybe a soldier, one who looked like Randolph Scott, shot it between the eyes after they dragged Christ away. Or maybe it waited in the shadow of the hill till everyone had gone, then snickered Christ alive and rode away with him toward the sunset where all the good guys go, a place of men and horses and all the risen lambs.

When he finally showed himself
he was a bird with ragged wings
and black crow feet. He landed
on her window sill, then hopped to the floor,
wings clattering like TV antennae
lowered from the roof and taken
to the nuisance grounds.
On one foot two toes were missing
and his chest was plucked bare,
goose-pimpled skin raw and scabby.
When he saw the look on her face,
he began to whine. "You think
I can help the way I look?
I like going where I'm not wanted?"
The woman felt sorry for him
till she remembered who he was.
"Shoo," she said, "Shoo,"
he limped toward her.
"I'll call the dog."
Death stopped. He coughed and coughed,
chest heaving as if his heart
were breaking out. "I don't feel well,"
he said. "I don't need all this trouble."
He hopped twice, his tail dragging
like a dirty broom across linoleum.
At the bedside table he raised
her cup of spittle, drank it down.
He unwound the bandages
from her throat and wiped his brow.
This close up, there was something
in his yellow eyes she found appealing.

They never blinked,
never closed, never had a chance
to stop looking at the world.
She threw back the covers and sat
on the bed for the first time in days.
Death put his wing around her
like an old-fashioned gentleman
offering his cape because
the night was cool. He said,
"It's not so bad, where we're going,
but you'll have to carry me a while.
My feet aren't what they used to be."
The woman felt her last
breath leave her body,
it hovered in the air between them,
then she stood and picked up Death.
He was light and suddenly no bigger
than a sparrow. If he spoke
she could no longer hear him.
He trembled in her hand,
the only warm thing against her flesh –
it was so cold. "It's okay,"
she tried to tell him.
"I won't hurt you."
She placed him gently in her mouth.
Her tongue seemed to be missing
and the inside of one cheek.
As she floated to the window
she was careful not to break
his small wings with her teeth.

The wave before it hits the shore
rises the way a cobra lifts

to music, beautiful and dangerous,
it falls, a long hiss across the sand,

Sis-i-utl, double-headed snake,
swallowing scale after scale.

Island View Beach. After the storm
logs raise their snouts, gleam

like mammals licking their backs. Easy
to imagine teeth and a tail flashing.

Here the winter solstice is the saint's
day of the drowned, all those

cups and celebration. The ocean
lisps an old refrain:

open your eyes
and the universe rolls in!

Room enough for sadness
but what of joy?

It needs more of you
to keep on going. Don't worry.

If you could not hold
so much the sea wouldn't ask.

* *

The sea has many houses,
ceilings moving up and down.

Whirlpools of stairways,
cellars of rust and bone:

instruments of navigation.
Déjà vu. Were you here before?

An octopus can be a window.
An eel, a sliding door.

Water is a form of braille,
your whole body reading.

* *

The moon has built its nest
fathoms deep. Li Po sleeps there,

his flask never full. Those are
pearls in the kelp bed,

those are eyes. They slide
from one side of the cod

to the other. Step out of the boat
the way you'd leave a pair of boots,

walk on water.
Is it not a miracle

to walk on earth?

＊＊

The boats drop off the edge
no matter what the new maps tell you.

The amnesia of oceans. Voices ride
the waves. *What have you forgotten*

that is so true? Day by day
ships return with their cargos

from the East. Is this enough to live
by? The smell of oranges and grapes

with dusty skin. Purple mouths
sing the sweetest, clumsy words

bruise the tongue. Blow into a reed,
a fish leaps, pulled by your line

of music. Caught, you go under.
Even here the sun's returning.

Travelling at the speed of darkness,
everything arrives at the light.

III

If I Call Stones Blue

(Ghazal Variations for the Spring Equinox)

I love words in the air balanced between mouths and ears I love the way they're smoke before they're stone.

– Patrick Friesen

Little sparrow, pray to the western wind,
invisible cowboy riding the waves.

Nothing to fear. The cat is a mummy.
Swaddled in linen in the Egyptian room

beside the Pharaoh's wife, under glass.
Centuries of stillness. Your long bathrobe

hangs on a hook behind our bedroom door.
No rustle, no hand in the pocket.

Our cat speaks in complete sentences. Get up.
I want my breakfast – beef, not salmon.

Early morning, the spoons on the white cloth
hold the sun's golden broth.

Two place settings.
                     Only one sits down.

      * *

Light slides across the sea like a boat
full of dreamers, their hair undone.

O my mad blind lover, where are you going
this cold morning with no dog to guide you?

The horse up the lane takes carrots from my hand
but won't let me touch him.

Don't put tulips and narcissus in the same vase,
says the flower-woman on the roadside.

Now you know everything you need to know.
I place the tulips by the coffee pot.

Companion planting. Old enamel stove
now you know it's spring.

     ✳ ✳

A pony in a red halter and beside him a tiger.
Candleholders made in India. Cut from tin.

Jack be nimble. We need a fire.
Strike a match, be quick! On the table

a book called *The Tremor of Racehorses.*
In translation from the Czech.

My new friend wants to learn another
name for cat. In any language.

Quick. *Le chat.* That's all I know.
The horse takes off with its fancy saddle,

a flame on its back. Tyger, tyger,
that fearful symmetry of fire, that tremor.

Another tongue – *Gato*! In the Mérida café
a black cat moving the air around our legs.

Under the table, the cups of fire,
a stray tiger made only from stripes.

⁂

The ants come in with the firewood.
Some longer than your little finger.

Lay your ear flat to the floor. Hear
their feet tapping as they disappear.

Under black umbrellas we strolled
Ross Bay Cemetery, searching for old numbers.

No luck. Everything has happened
too soon. The grass here never yellows.

A live string swings across the floor.
Carpenter ants. Leather aprons.

The bread's in the oven.
Open the door. Tap, tap, tap.

Just the rain or a fingernail
testing the crust to see if it's done.

The linoleum's cold. Where is their graveyard?
They keep moving it; no one knows why.

＊＊

My first winter without snow.
The sea full of melting men.

Eyes made out of coal.
Where are the blue shadows cast

by the brain, the sparrow's hieroglyphs?
Who cares but me? The loon in the bay

followed me from Saskatchewan.
How do I know? Listen,

his call is syllables.
Ululation. *Waskesiu.*

**

Across the bay Mount Baker
has returned from its migration.

Hitching a ride, so many white swans
high on its peak, their wings at rest.

Crows never leave. Another sign
of spring: the rubber hand and arm

of a troll doll I find in the grass,
the foot of some extinct sea-bird.

In the blue-carp bowl from Chinatown,
stones. A quick lick (salt!)

and they change colour.
Everything changes but the heart.

Something doesn't bloom,
doesn't blossom.

* *

Keep a weather journal.
Write: first day of spring.

Write: the naked gardens of my skin.
Write: no buds on this tree.

**

The tulip tree: a candelabra.
Abracadabra! Each evening we wait for

the candles to be lit. A crow flies by
with a stick in its mouth. Remember

the new yellow pencil, its significant
weight between your fingers. Wait, that's fall!

Every hour a different boat goes by.
I never see them coming back.

The whales have returned to Tofino.
Why do I sit inside, looking out?

Weather. Or not.
The dried flowers on the sill

all winter are dull with dust. Out of
season. Burn them in the tulip tree.

Where is that dog who was supposed to
pick you up?

Rolling in the daffodils.
Old Yeller.

＊＊

Given this much, this much
of anything. Sea, sea, see!

Earthly delight. Abundance, anemone.
The face of the middle-aged woman

is sprinkled with freckles. Red-brown.
Cinnamon. The child's still there.

George from the reserve says
the herring are back! You can tell

by the way the birds are flying.
With my little eye, I didn't notice.

    * *

It's a fluke! Hah! Chance or whale?
The hummingbird leaves nothing to it.

Gathers spider webs to build its nest.
Threads of dew. Eggs so small

a hen would laugh. Though it's the cockerel
we think of. Laughing its head off.

The chopping block. The axe's silver grin.
Ask anyone. When the whale went by

I was humming "On a Clear Day" and hanging
the wash on the line. All the birds

stopped singing. It needed that much silence
to move through. In one eye and out

the other. The last laugh is always
best. It takes all season.

        ✳ ✳

An eagle lands on the beach.
I ask my Cree friend what to do.

Run out with a handful of tobacco.
Gone! But the crows tell me where he is

from tree to tree. Your rosewood pipe
beside the driftwood, bowl still warm.

Fingers and talons. The broken cup
still holds water.

In the bay the herring spawn
under a roe-coloured moon.

**

You whispered in my deaf ear, the other
pressed into the pillow. Tell me

you love me. The wren outside the window
chatters at 5 a.m. I don't know, bird!

I don't know where your wife's
gone off to. There's never enough

bacon to go around. This is one thing
I'm sure of. Beer in the batter,

carrots in the cake, beauty in the
sea's orange stars. Today a letter

arrived from the cat. I'm okay
in Saskatoon without you though

I prefer your lap. He always says
the right thing, that cat.

    ❋ ❋

The maple is the first to gather light,
then the spruce, then the hemlock.

Let's make wine from grape
hyacinths! Our mouths so blue.

Only blue words
can fly through the air

faster than thought.
If I call stones blue

Flaubert writes,
that's exactly what they are.

      * *

Dust falling from the fir boughs
where the crow lands

is not dust but pollen. Imagine that!
All your pipes have disappeared.

Are you going somewhere? My favourite
lamp in this cabin is a Snow-White Dwarf

in a red jacket and tall yellow hat.
The bulb grows from his head. Eureka!

The gull on the roof across the way
holds a star in his beak. Red Dog. Aldebaran.

Pig-glass and a shell, the one
Botticelli rode in from the sea.

Froth in a tankard. A camellia broad
and red as a drunkard's face. Here,

I've found your slippers. They're so full
of holes they're empty. What to do?

The long journey. Take care of your feet.
How down to earth I feel by the huge water.

    **

The man next door leads a blind dog
down the lane. You can hear her sniffing

before you see her. Crocuses grow tall
here, four inches, their eyes

wide open. A wave leapt to shore today
and carried off a man.

A prey of salt and water.
What was he thinking?

Gardens everywhere
even when you cannot see them.

A widow walks the beach looking for
a pair of shoes, a word, a brown felt hat.

An eyewitness says he waved
just before he disappeared.

No loved one in the harbour
to see him off.

⁕⁕

A tugboat pulls a house, two-storeys,
windows boarded up.

The whole kit and caboodle
towed across the water. *Quo vadis?*

Who's the captain? The housewife
in the kitchen baking bread.

The gulls know it. Or is it herring
they're after?

What an address!
Whale road, eel path, coral crescent.

You can reach me
at Half-Moon Bay when the moon is full.

In that other place
it's the sky that's on the move.

     **

Two swans float past
in the early morning, return late afternoon.

You can set your clocks.
According to the book

they shouldn't be here.
At dawn they carry all the light

in their white feathers.
Mute swans. Soul catchers.

Messengers from that other moon
on the bottom of the sea.

Two strange hearts
                    drift in feather boats

across your sight. No sound.
A flute made out of bone

when the breath
                    stops.

IV

Turning the Earth

The way is open, it is paved with stones;
They are the fallen eyes of angels.

– Gwendolyn MacEwen

On the white planet everything is crème de la
crème, palely glistening or glowing with
the confidence of old stoves, enamel
scrubbed to a hard shine. There,
mountains are ice and mica shot with light.
Milkweed grows high in the meadows
and in the valleys, apples,
turned inside out,
hang like startled moons from the ghostly
limbs of trees.

       The people who pick them
stare sightless through the whites of their eyes
and do everything by touch. Wonderful lovers,
they know one another
piece by puzzling piece, the body divided
into its disparate beauties,
separately voluptuous,
nothing whole.

       The earthly eye, even
with the aid of telescope and satellite
cannot find them – nor their illuminated
mountains high in space, their orchards
ripe with moons,
their lost marble cities –
the people of the white planet
blending as they do

               into colour's absence
the way a leopard in the forests
assumes the dappled darkness and the light.

Under clouds which never bruise
their breath turns crystalline,
colourless stars that fall and fall,
covering the dark side of our world
with galaxies of snow.

Under the earth
radishes are the first
to light their lanterns,
spreading a watery glow
throughout the garden.

The star-nosed mole
who tunnels through the dark
thinks he is the chosen one,
all his paths suddenly
diffused with light.

Potatoes build their constellations
row on row like a child
trying to understand
the solar system,
each planet connected
by a string. Above,
tomatoes draw
what little warmth there is
inside, wax round
and glossy on their stems.

Digging to the surface
for the first time
the mole thinks he's found
another world – a sky
of moons, green and red,
each one growing larger
in his dark myopic eyes,
eclipsing all he knows
of earth.

The woman who drums in her garden
to scare away the magpies (a bodhran
drum, a bongo, sometimes a kettle drum
with sticks) has actually taught them
how to dance. They began with little
hops and head bobs, nodding yes, yes, yes,
to fearlessness and mischief.

This held a certain fascination
but after several days as if they sensed
the possibility of boredom, the hard
beads of a pellet gun glinting in her eyes,
each leaned forward, raised one foot,
tapped the taut blue air,
lowered the foot, then raised the other,
on and on in a circle dance. One learned
to clap its wings, another twirled on toes,
head thrown back like a figure skater.

She told her neighbours
she drummed to scare the magpies.
Certainly there were none in their gardens –
how plump the peas this year, how sweet
the songbird's singing! No one thought
to climb the maple, peer over her high fence.

One night next door, the smallest boy
said he heard another sound,
a dark under-rhythm,
a different sort of knowing
that moved beyond a woman's hands.

No one ever listened to him,
a strange and lonely boy who kept
a gopher in his pocket,
who caught crickets
to release them in the pantry
till he found one who would sing.

Towards summer's end, her drums inside,
all she had to do was sit in the garden,
sometimes the boy beside her,
and the birds dropped down without a cry.
On a patch of flattened peas and leaves of cabbage,
they stepped, flapped, and shuffled
to the muffled beating of her heart.

It was only when the swan
felt himself inside the girl
he finally understood
what it meant to be a god –
that passion like a star
exploding, that absolute
abuse of power. That's all
we know of him. As a swan

he never appeared again
but the girl who was taken
was left behind. Indeed,
she felt the heavens in her womb
but had no word for it
and wondered what to say.

Who'd believe it was a swan?
No different in appearance
from the wild ones
floating on the lake.
Like lanterns made of feathers
they lit the water and the water changed
as she was changed by something
more than them and less.

These were the swans
her brothers caught with nets.
Her mother stuck them
in the throat with a silver pin
so they would bleed
and could be plucked and roasted.

Tied by their feet they hung in rows,
long necks drooping above pools
of blood, feathers streaked with red
like the flesh of her inner thighs.
All of them so anonymous and soft,
she pitied them
and would not eat their wildness.

She had thought him wounded
when he dropped brilliant from the sky
and stumbled with a swan's true
awkwardness on land toward her.
She tried to hide him in her skirts
to keep him from her mother.

Now she was the wounded one,
the village crazy girl
with the story of the swan,
a god inside her,
while the dead ones hung,
their necks feather clappers
in a clear glass bell
only she could see, a bell
fragile as the body of a girl
before she's rung.

> *Two women shall be grinding at the mill; the one shall be*
> *taken, and the other left.*
> — Matthew 24:41

She saw her sister spill her bowl,
then rise toward a cloud
as she'd seen her many times
stretch on tiptoes
to reach the hides of lambs
drying cleanly in the sun, morning
heavy with the scent of lanolin.

If the villagers had known their god
would choose between these two,
they could have guessed. The smaller
sister seemed all spirit, no rounded hips
or belly, no waxing breasts that made up
what a woman was. Hardly anything
to lift to heaven.

Not knowing what else to do,
the one left behind
began to grind the corn,
hands covered with golden dust
like pollen or what a soul might
leave when it ascends.
She hoped there still was time
before the second coming,
the plagues and conflagration,
time to grind enough to make a loaf,
a last one for her lover.

She could see his shepherd's hands,
breaking the bread in half,
steam rising from its heart
like her body's heat
when they lay together in dirty straw
far from her father's terrible eyes,
he who loved her sister
as fathers often loved the girl
but not the woman she'd become.

The last thing she saw of her,
rising out of sight,
was the bottom of her feet
which had never worn shoes,
suddenly unlined,
and from the cloud that seemed to carry her
they wore the shine of flesh
lit up from loving.

The sister left on earth
couldn't help but think
she might be the chosen one,
her bare feet gripping the muscles
in his calves once more,
above her his belly rippling
like rows of ripened barley.

Even now as the sky darkened
over the houses of the village
was she not blessed? The millstone
turning one thing into another
before her eyes.

Of all the animals it was the snails
I loved best. There was beauty in the others,
the foxes' flaming tails, the eyes
of owls, pools of pure light
where I would have bathed if not
for all the water lapping,
my mind an island of eroding sand.

The salamanders, too, with their grace.
Their fingers seemed to stroke green
music from the air. Cats were my familiars,
perhaps too close for me
to remember my earthly delight
in the small hairs inside their ears
like the ones that guided bees into
the foxglove blooms drowning in my garden.

After a week at sea the air smelled
of rotting pomegranate and banana,
the autumn scent of hay, waste that grew
on wooden planks like strange
misshapen mushrooms slick with flies.

When I watched from the deck
almost all I had loved swept away,
it was not my husband
but the snails who comforted me. Each
came aboard with its house intact,
its room devoid of altars, of reminiscence,
the small things a boy might save
to remind him of the earth.

Like a woman the snail tucked itself
inside its shadow, slid on silence,
whatever it said to its mate no one could hear
nor the cries when they came together
on the underside of leaves.

As the ark sailed on my strange imagining,
and dove after dove fell from the sky,
I built my shell: one door, one window, stairs
leading nowhere because there'd been no stars
for days. Rain hammered the waves,
shattered the faces that stared at me
with the eyes of dolphins.
I began to see my husband's penis
as a snail's silver horn. Without words
I welcomed it under the eye of his angry god
whose spittle had drowned the world.

When my husband slept I slipped into
my own domed emptiness
and for no reason I could understand,
I licked the snails one by one
and placed them on his eyelids,
living coins.

I can phone him any time, he says,
though most mornings he's in the garden.
The days are sunny now, mid-July,
and there's weeding to be done. I'm sick
with worry and a thousand miles away.
He says he's getting better, the infection
in his eyes is clearing up though he forgot
his allergy to sulpha. Now he can see
well enough to weed between the lupines.
When I hang up, not home for a week
or more, weariness washes over me.
The way I feel is like the end of love
when you're the one who's been jilted
and nothing you can say or do will stop
what's going on. On top of that,
the cat is home from the vet's,
a tube sticking from his stomach.
My stoic love with troubled eyes
pushes food into him three times a day
with a syringe. The cat has begun to bite.
I've written on a stone and buried it
in a potato field so I won't think
about them anymore. For a week I have to
find a way to keep on going. At the end of love
everything around you seems so tender,
so absolute. When the red-crested
chipping sparrow throws back his head and sings
outside my window, his whole body
trembles inside the song.

I love your feet. Father Phillip can't
believe it, tucked inside his socks
just delivered from the laundryroom
this note, *I love your feet,* then
three *x*'s, double *o*'s. Halfway across
the grounds to tell the Abbot,
he thinks better of it, remembers
an hour ago when he'd squealed on
Brother Harold, the disgusting
butt floating in the toilet bowl,
the Abbot saying, "Lighten up,"
as if they were teenagers
or part of a commercial for selling cigarettes.
I love your feet. Could it be Agnes
the laundry woman who laughs too loud
and slaps him on the back as if he were choking
though he hasn't choked in years,
forty chews a mouthful and lots of tea.
I love your feet. Could it be the young
pony-tailed novitiate who picks weeds
from the roadside and calls them flowers,
who replaces turnips with columbines
in the old monks' garden, carrots with lupines
taller than the chapel candle stand?
Is it the reflexologist who drives from the city
once a week on the Abbot's invitation,
bounces around the grounds without a bra
and pounds the brothers' soles with wooden hammers?
I love your feet. Yesterday, his turn to do the dishes,
the cook reached in the sink to grab a pot
and touched his hand beneath the bubbles.

Sure it was deliberate, he'd jumped
as if she'd thrown an eel into the water,
fleshy and electric. Someone loves his *feet*.
Could that someone know he wears socks
in the shower, and in winter nights,
the sheets so short, wears socks to bed?
Could they know when he lived alone
before the abbey, he married each pair
with a safety pin so the machine wouldn't
swallow one and leave a single
he couldn't match? *I love your feet*.
After vespers he makes himself
look at them, naked on the bed,
innocent and pale, like something on its way
to being something else. The vein
that runs from toe to ankle could be
a fat blue worm, in another's eyes,
the river of Jerusalem. *I love your feet*.
He waits for laundry day with dread,
with sweet anticipation,
the way the chubby, hopeful boy he was
drew a line through each square
on the Wheat Pool calendar
and walked the dirt road to the mailbox
once, twice, three times a day,
fingers trembling when he lowered the flag
and opened the little door, expecting
the secret kit from Charles Atlas.
I love your feet. Three *x*'s, double *o*'s.
Maybe he should pin a note
inside his dirty socks, but what to say?
He walks more lightly about the abbey
as if on water, raises his robes
a little higher when he climbs the stairs,

stands with one foot slightly forward
like the beautiful David poised in stone.
When he finds Brother Harold's cigarettes
forgotten beside the cookie tin,
he tucks a note inside the pack,
I love your mouth. Already he is planning
what to slip in the pocket of the Abbot's
clean pyjamas, what to write in pencil
on the cotton gloves of the novitiate
whose fingers green from gardening
smell like flowers
even when the season's done.

He had a good wife, he said,
she did not complete his sentences.

A man and a woman talking together.
A man, a woman, and a cat, his huge

alphabet of smells – the hair
rising on the back of his neck,

musk of a strange poem or cat?
At dusk my hands roam over you,

graze with soft slow mouths.
Saith Isaiah, *My people,*

all flesh is grass. Meadow
fescue, gold foxtail, and plume.

She had a good husband,
she said. Complete this sentence:

he did not. . . .

  **

On his thirteenth year the cat
falls in love with fire.

He lies on the rug and listens,
ears diaphanous. In winter

light becomes a tunnel, two yellow
ropes thrown into the dark.

Anchors, but we're moving
in a fast car, windows frosted up.

When he's in love (or is it
just a need for salt) the cat

licks my fingers. His tongue,
a rough flame, makes me

transparent. I can see
the bones shining through.

* *

You say he is older,
I deny it. Your sentence

needs finishing. A fine sheen
on the oak table, a warp in the leaf.

All that work and I never
noticed, my hands moving

beyond the peripheries
of thought, uncovering the grain,

memory's dense knots. Where's
the cat, mouth full of feathers,

of fire? Ashes fall on the old
poet's jacket. Before the reading

his wife pinned a note
to his lapel. *Fly*, it says.

Noun or verb? A good wife,
she lets him find the answer.

If a woman could become
a horse, she would be one:
her long, slender forelegs,
the finely shaped head
with its tangled mane, the soft
wrinkled mouth you long to touch,
say, *Speak, and I will feed you.*

People gather at the roadside
when she runs, though she chooses
the gravel of the country
where everyone lives close
as the sky allows,
its blue insistent fever
burning thin her bones.

If Zeus looked down and wanted her,
he would greet her as a horse,
not force himself upon her
with a blow of wings. He'd lope
along her side, nickering and neighing,
nuzzling her thigh with dappled mouth
until she understood his tongue.

No matter what,
there'd be no Helen, no creature
with a god's gleam about it,
licked by stars. She is past
the age of bearing, her eyes spin
webs of wrinkles across her skin.

Days when her body is on fire,
legs and arms tinder in the wind,
she runs past meadow mares.
They toss their heads and race
along the fenceline, foals rocking
in sorrel cradles,
hooves soft as rubber. She can feel
every muscle shrink and stretch,
the ebbing power of her womb.

What language does she dream in now
in the middle of this changing?

Free of the moon's complicity,
her body flares and trembles,
skin smelling of dusty grass.
Drenched with sweat, she tosses
back her hair, thick and golden,
her own warm light
falling all around her.

I stand across from the man I haven't seen
in fifteen years. He is my husband.
I look him in the eye.
I touch his thin brown fingers.
It is now fifteen years ago.
The dog we raised from a pup
turns in a circle on the doorstep.
She has dug her way out of the earth
as she used to dig in,
tunnelling after gophers.
There is dirt in her mouth and eyes.
She shakes her beautiful ears
and the flies that laid eggs in her skull
lift from her head, drift to the apples
unripening, turning back
into blossoms on the boughs.
I am about to speak.
The letter I wrote on the shore of Lake Winnipeg
when I ran away from him
returns to that place, unopened,
ink flowing backward into my pen.
The car coasts in reverse
down the gravel lane to our house.
I retrace my steps across the grass,
toe to heel   toe to heel
in slow motion over and over
rehearse the words
I never said fifteen years before.
He waits for me to speak, the door half open.
On the step, her collar too big,

the dog dreams back to her first rabbit,
her legs running and running
in that other world.

At the end of her marriage
she stands on the edge of the cliff,
and with others who have gathered,
watches a bull moose swimming out to sea.
He plunges, pulls himself up the waves,
sinks, towers with a fierceness
none of them can understand.
Someone yells, "Turn around, turn around!"
but she knows it's too late.
Her neck grows tired as if it's
her head bearing the weight, antlers
sprouting from the brain's thick forest.
The moose moves further and further out,
the terns above her head
bigger now than what diminishes
across the water. In all that blue
she tries to imagine an island
floating on the waves, a foothold,
a place of rest,
but nothing grows beyond her tenderness.
If she'd seen this a year ago
would anything have changed?
Someone must speak, try to
make sense of things before they end,
as the sea washes and washes the shore below,
bringing nothing back.

The worst thing about
a horse bite is the horse

can't change his mind,
can't open his mouth,

release the flesh
until his jaws clamp shut.

Once the pain starts
you know it has to

get worse before
it stops.

FIRE BREATHER
for Patrick

When I drank what you gave me I burned
my mouth. So much fire on these lips.
You should have told me.

I was used to tasting your homemade soups
with a wooden spoon, testing the flavour,
the windows steamed so I couldn't see out.

Add more barley, I'd say, or those red spices
from the Nile. You'd save everything, even
tongues, hearts, and pickerel cheeks.

We could be in Japan, our shoes off all the time.
Under my fingers your flesh gives like grass mats,
Blue-Eyed or Brome. Oh, you're a quiet one.

Nothing to show, but inside enough heat
to light the tallow candles you bought
from the butcher who gives you soup bones for free.

After I take you in my mouth I can blow flames
across a room. A strange bed for us to lie in,
all these ashes and my feet still cold.

Naked, you bring me water
(yes, I'm thirsty!)
in your mouth,
place it over mine
so I taste you
in the cold rivers of the city.

Sometimes my love for you
is a boat I ride,
soundlessly,
never sure where I'm going
as if East and West
had nothing to do
with the sun,
were simply words
tattooed on the arms
of a sailor lost
at sea.

I can't believe this
rainy season. The small
hairs on your belly
swirl in one direction
like grass at the bottom
of a stream. Adrift

in a boat that holds
a restless cargo
I'm still thirsty,
the only water I can drink
is from your mouth.

A SABBATH HYMN

A Sabbath hymn from below rose
with the shouts of hairy men in the showers.
— Yehuda Amichai

After reading Yehuda Amichai
translated from the Hebrew,
the holy tongue, I can't stop
thinking of hairy men in showers.
At least six of them in a row
soaping their hard bodies
with the slap and muscle of men
in groups. They scrub from hairy
chest to hairy thigh
with fierceness and rejoicing.
Mounds of bubbles blink
on downy bellies,
bald, flaccid penises
where their mothers made them
wash and wash, the scrotums innocent
and shiny as new plums after rain.
What do they shout above the shower's drill?
"Hallelujah! All men! Whisker, beard, ram's wool!"
Water like a woman's hands, like a god's
tongue creating man from foam,
like the razor of a small-town barber,
smooths, licks, and scrapes the lather off.

I'm the one you've fucked
across the continent,
sometimes in the back seat
of your Fairlane Ford,
sometimes in the basements
of your friends. I always left
before breakfast while you
flirted with the wife
and fried the bacon,
your fingerprints
and smoke all over me.

I first met you in Winnipeg.
Wearing my mother's fur
over my naked skin,
my breasts sweet as apricots.
I called you *Mister*
when you drove me home,
your poems
singing in my head.

Off the 401
in the dashboard light
I showed you my scribbler
where I'd written you
in pencil and kissed
the pages red. You put
my hand in your lap
under the wheel, said,
This one's for you.
The radio was playing

"It's a Heartbreak,"
Bonnie Tyler's throat
full of Grand Marnier and come.
I was chewing Certs so hard
I cracked a tooth. See,
I never got it fixed.

A year ago in Montreal
you snorted my skin
like uncut coke
until your nostrils bled.
Weeks before, knowing
you'd be in town,
I wore designer jeans
in the bathtub
so they'd be tight enough
to peel off
the way you'd strip
a peach.

Okanagan's a word
I've become familiar with.
I wash my hair in the smell
of pears and apples,
wear a t-shirt
that says *Cherryland*
so you'll think
it's my first time
when I close my eyes
and moan.

The night your wife walked in,
in Calgary, me naked on your lap
in the chair we'd bucked

across the kitchen,
you said I was the one
who started it and we'd
just met. I left my clothes,
even my new boots behind,
and ran into the street,
wet with you and cold.
A boy lent me his hockey sweater
to cover up. All I had
to do was jack him off
and he gave me a lift,
the face of an Indian
on my chest and back.

That afternoon in Halifax
we made it
on a fishing boat,
legs alive with scales,
your face red as a lobster
when you came.
Who smells of fish? I said
and laughed, the wooden
traps jumping around us.

Now I'm waiting at Mile Zero,
my yellow slicker
a lantern in the rain.
I can feel you moving
toward me like a cowboy
in a paperback, his horse
smelling home.

Admit it. You just can't
stay away – I'm the music

in your mouth, your love
of cunt and whisky,
my whole body fits you
like a lambskin glove,
oh Mister, where do we go
from here?

The only way to tell you is to write
this down, our lives a journal
with notes about the weather, perhaps
a grocery list and appointments never kept
because the sparrows sing for seeds
in our apple tree, and the spider
at the centre of her web demands
your poet's eye to hold her still.

You are fifty-five today. I must find
as many ways to tell you, as many places
on your body for my tongue to touch.
Last spring, our first on the Coast,
you said you'd never had a better birthday
and wondered why. You'd been working
in the garden, turning the damp earth.
On the prairies it would still be frozen
nine feet down. For a body to be buried,
the ground is set on fire, bundles of straw smoking.
Birthdays always bring the old deaths back.

From the window, I watch you digging
in one of the sweaters you'll wear
till the wool is worn thin and I insist
on putting it away. I save each one
as if your mother who knitted them
wanted what little warmth is left
to make something smaller, a sweater
for the boy who curled inside her belly
as she waited in the spring for the pale
buds of fingers to unfurl and bloom.

Earlier in bed, your hands cold from the soil,
I wept after I cried out, not knowing why.
Fifteen years together and some days
there's such pleasure in our bodies
as they move through the seasons, far
from the beauty they were born to. Now
they shine like parchment, worn by fingers,
by the spittle on the thumb as we turn
a page. We read each other, nearsightedly,
hands and tongues and even toes find where
the skin gives way. Since I cannot say
it right, for you today I must try

to keep this journal. Write:
March 26, and a little cold.
Write: Overnight the plum tree
has become one blossom. Write:
The days are getting longer
because my lover in the garden
turns and turns the earth.

Acknowledgements

Some of the poems in this book have appeared in the following magazines in Canada: *Descant, Border Crossings, Grain, Prism International, The Malahat Review, Room of One's Own, Poetry Canada Review, The Fiddlehead, Canadian Literature, The New Quarterly, Prairie Fire*, and *Event*; in *The Globe and Mail*; and in the anthologies *Because You Were a Stranger, Modern Poems in English, Beyond Borders, Witness to Wilderness: The Clayoquot Sound Anthology, Take This Waltz*, and *bite to eat place: The Redwood Coven Press Food Anthology*. "A Good Day to Start a Journal" was broadcast on CBC's "Morningside."

In the United States several have appeared in: *The Southern Review, Prairie Schooner, The Atlanta Review, The New Quarterly*, and *Nimrod*.

The ghazal sequence "If I Call Stones Blue" was first published as a limited edition chapbook, *Eye Witness*, by Reference West Press in 1993.

"When I Come Again to My Father's House" was written after a poem by Galway Kinnell called "Memories of My Father." The title and first line are variations of one of his lines. The story of the stallion in "Dressage" I heard from the Welsh poet, Gillian Clarke. In "The Sea at the End of the World" the italicized question is Robert Penn Warren's.

I would like to thank Donna Bennett for her editing demands, Patrick Lane for his advice, love, and support, and the Saskatchewan Artists'/Writers' Colony Committee for providing a space to write.